KT-514-144

017

C152655622

Sally Morgan

FRANKLIN WATTS
LONDON • SYDNEY

© 2005 Franklin Watts
First published in 2005
by Franklin Watts
96 Leonard Street
London EC2A 4XD

Franklin Watts Australia
45-51 Huntley Street
Alexandria NSW 2015

Produced for Franklin Watts by
White-Thomson Publishing Ltd
210 High Street
Lewes BN7 2NH

Editor: Rachel Minay
Designed by: Tinstar Design Ltd
Picture research: Morgan Interactive Ltd
Consultant: Frank Blackburn
Printed in: China

**British Library Cataloguing
in Publication Data**
A CIP catalogue record for this book is
available from the British Library.

ISBN: 0 7496 6067 8

KENT
ARTS & LIBRARIES

C152655622

Acknowledgements
The publishers would like to thank
the following for permission to
reproduce these photographs:

Corbis
9 (Roger Wilmshurst);

Ecoscene
11, 12 (Robin Redfern), 13 (William
Middleton), 15, 18, 21 (Robert Pickett),
25, 28 (Robin Redfern);

Nature Picture Library
FC, 1 (Kevin Keatley), 4–5 (Jose B Ruiz), 6,
7 (Andrew Cooper), 8 (Colin Seddon), 10,
14, 16 (Kevin Keatley), 17 (Colin Seddon),
19 (Kevin Keatley), 20 (Paul Hobson),
22 (Andrew Parkinson), 23 (Dietmar Nill),
24 (Kevin Keatley), 26 (Paul Hobson),
27 (Andrew Cooper), 29 (Kevin Keatley).

Every effort has been made to contact copyright
holders of any material reproduced in this book.
Any omissions will be rectified in subsequent
printings if notice is given to the publishers.

Contents

The badger

The badger is a well-known British animal. It has a distinctive black and white striped face.

Badgers are powerful animals about the size of a medium-sized dog. The male badger is called a boar, the female is a sow and the young are called cubs. They live in an underground home called a sett.

The body of the badger is covered in black and white hairs, which give the animal a dark-grey appearance when seen from a distance. Its chest and front paws are black. Most noticeable is its black and white striped head and white ears.

VITAL **STATISTICS**

- ▸ *The body of a badger is about 75 cm from head to tail.*
- ▸ *Its tail is 15 cm long.*
- ▸ *It weighs between 8–9 kg in spring and 11–12 kg in autumn.*
- ▸ *Its life span is between four and five years, although a few may live as long as 15 years.*
- ▸ *The Latin name for the badger is Meles meles.*

The badger has a powerful, barrel-shaped body with a coat of stiff hairs.

short legs ending in long claws

The badger is a mammal

The badger belongs to a group of animals called mammals. Most female mammals give birth to live young and feed their young with milk.

black and white head

body covered in long black and white hairs

5

Reproduction

Badgers mate any time between February and October.

It doesn't matter when the mating takes place – the cubs are always born between January and March. This is because the sow can delay the start of her pregnancy to make sure her cubs are born at a time of year when there is plenty of food.

The sow is pregnant for about seven weeks. She gives birth to a litter of two or three cubs in an underground home called a sett.

The cubs will spend the first two months of life in the sett so the sow has to keep it clean.

The cubs play with each other while they are in the nursery chamber.

Newborn cubs

The newborn badger cubs are covered in grey silky hairs. Often the dark stripes on the face are already visible. Each cub is about 12 cm long and weighs between 75 and 130 g. The cubs' eyes are closed for the first five weeks. This isn't a problem as they're living in a dark sett and can't see much anyway! They rely on their senses of smell and hearing.

ANIMAL **FACTS**

▶ *Only one in every three cubs will survive until its first birthday. Some cubs will starve while others may die from disease or be run over on roads.*

Growing up

The cubs grow quickly and once they are eight weeks old they are ready to venture outside of their sett.

Cub food

The cubs feed on their mother's milk until they are 12 weeks old. Then they start to eat solid food. They follow their mother when she goes off to feed and learn which foods to eat. By the time they are 15 weeks old, the cubs are ready to hunt for food on their own.

This four-month-old cub is on its own, looking for food.

Badger cubs come out of the sett at dusk to feed and play.

Playing together

The cubs love playing together. They often play-fight and chase each other. A favourite game is 'tag' in which the cubs chase each other around a tree trunk or in and out of holes. Play is very important as it helps the cubs to develop coordination and it strengthens their muscles.

By autumn, the cubs are nearly as big as the adults. They do not play as much and spend a lot of time eating.

ANIMAL **FACTS**

▶ *By early May, the cubs have grown rapidly and each weighs about 3 kg.*

Where do badgers live?

Badgers are found all over Britain. They are common in south-west England but quite rare in East Anglia and parts of Scotland.

Badger habitats

Badgers' favourite habitats are woodland, grassland and hedgerows. In particular, they like wooded areas that lie close to farmland. Badgers do not like flat areas or land that is very wet. Gently sloping land is ideal for building a sett that will stay dry.

ANIMAL **FACTS**

▶ *There are between 250,000 and 310,000 badgers in Britain living in about 80,000 family groups.*

Woodland provides badgers with lots of food and places to dig out their setts.

Badgers raid dustbins at night, looking for food.

Badgers live in cities

In recent years, badgers have moved into urban gardens and parks. They have learnt that there is food to be found in gardens. Badgers help gardeners by eating slugs and snails in the garden. Badger setts are found in parks and on waste ground.

animal CLUES

You can attract badgers into your garden at night by putting out some water. They love unsalted peanuts so scatter some on the lawn and watch the badgers sniff them out.

Badger setts

Badgers live in an underground maze of tunnels and chambers called a sett. Each family group has one main sett and a number of smaller setts that they use from time to time.

Underground home

The underground tunnels can stretch a long way, in some cases as far as 30 metres. At the end of each tunnel is a chamber that is used for sleeping or raising cubs. Every few metres, a tunnel is widened so that badgers can pass each other. Most setts have several entrance holes and tunnels that link up with each other.

A large sett may have as many as 100 entrances and have been occupied by badgers for well over 100 years.

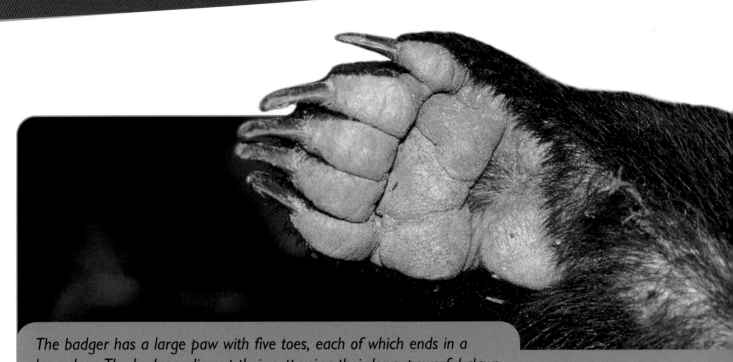

The badger has a large paw with five toes, each of which ends in a long claw. The badgers dig out their sett using their long, powerful claws.

Favourite places for setts

Badgers like to dig their setts where the ground is soft and easy to dig, for example sandy soil. They do not like digging in sticky clay. They like slopes, such as the side of a hill or a bank. A sloping site means water drains away and the sett stays dry.

ANIMAL **FACTS**

▸ One well-studied badger sett in the Cotswolds has 12 entrances and more than 300 m of tunnels. The badgers had probably dug out 25,000 kg of soil to make their sett.

animal CLUES

Look out for badger setts. A good place to find one is in a small woodland clearing or the bank of a hedge. The ground around the entrance is free of vegetation and there may be a pile of freshly dug soil nearby.

Badgers live in groups

Badgers live in small family groups called clans. A clan is typically made up of an adult boar, several sows and their cubs.

Badger clans

The adult boar controls the group. There is usually only one adult boar in the clan, so young boars have to leave once they are fully grown. They may join another clan if the adult boar has died, or live alone. Most of the young sows stay with their clan. They are ready to have their own cubs when they are 15 months old.

ANIMAL **FACTS**

▸ *The size of a badger's territory depends on the habitat and the amount of food available. A territory can be as small as 0.15 sq km or as large as 15 sq km.*

This is a large clan with a number of sows and older cubs. They are foraging for food.

Badgers tend to use the same paths each night.

Badgers live in territories

Each clan lives in a particular territory. They find all their food here and move around at night, following well-trodden paths. If a badger from one clan wanders into another clan's territory, there may be a fight. Badgers have very powerful jaws and sharp teeth and they can inflict serious injuries. Sometimes members of the same clan may fight, usually when too many badgers are in the clan and there is not enough food to go round.

animal CLUES

You can tell if a badger is using a path by looking for tufts of badger hairs caught on fences and barbed wire. You can also place a stick by the path with some double-sided tape attached to it. As the badger brushes past, hairs get stuck on the tape.

Badger food

Badgers are grouped with meat-eating carnivores such as dogs, wolves and weasels. However, badgers are really omnivores because they eat both plants and animals.

Feeding on earthworms

The badger's favourite food is the earthworm. They search for earthworms on grassland, hoovering them up as quickly as possible. They have to be quick as the earthworms are very sensitive to vibrations and may escape if disturbed.

ANIMAL **FACTS**

▸ *On a good night a badger can eat several hundred earthworms.*

This young badger has found a slug and is smelling it carefully.

canine

This is the skull of an adult badger. Badgers have 38 teeth. They have four long canines, which they use to grip food and defend themselves.

Finding other food

When there are fewer earthworms around, badgers feed on other foods such as fruits, roots and bulbs. They also eat small animals such as voles, mice, young rabbits and insects; for example, badgers eat the dung beetles that are found living near cowpats!

Badgers eat wasp larvae too. They dig out wasp nests and break open the top to get at the larvae inside. Their thick hair protects them from wasp stings. In winter they may feed on dead animals because other food is in short supply.

Senses

Badgers are nocturnal. This means they are active at night. They spend the day resting in their setts and emerge at dusk.

Poor eyesight

The badger is a very cautious animal and it does not rush out of its sett. It stands at the entrance, sniffing and listening for signs of danger. Badgers are active in the dark so they do not need to have particularly good eyesight. They have small eyes and cannot see in colour, just in black and white, and shades of grey. They cannot see details but can detect movement.

This badger is standing very still and alert. It is listening carefully for any sound of danger.

ANIMAL **FACTS**

▸ *Sadly as many as 50,000 badgers die on British roads each year. They are often blinded by headlights and unable to get out of the way of cars.*

Finding food

The badger's senses of hearing and smell are far more important than its eyesight. A badger relies on its sense of smell to find its way around and to find tasty roots and insect larvae in the soil.

Sshhh!

Anybody watching badgers at night has to be extremely quiet. Badgers can hear the rustle of clothing from a distance and are able to smell perfume and other scents.

A badger's sense of smell is many times better than ours and badgers can smell things that people cannot.

Badger communication

Badgers communicate with each other using smell and sound.

Recognising scent

Badgers in the same clan recognise each other by scent. The badger produces a strong-smelling liquid, called musk, from a gland under its tail. One badger marks another by backing on to it with its tail raised to smear on some musk. Badgers also leave their scent on the ground to help them find their way around their territory at night.

Badgers that are injured and treated at an animal hospital may lose their smell. When they are returned to their clan they are not recognised and may be chased away. Injured badgers have to be treated as quickly as possible and returned before their scent is lost.

This badger has found an interesting scent on the tree and is sniffing it carefully.

ANIMAL **FACTS**

▶ *Badgers are protected by law, which means it is illegal to harm a badger or damage or block their setts.*

Badger sounds

Badgers make a variety of sounds such as squeals, snorts, grunts and sniffs. Adults growl or bark as a warning and purr when they are happy. Badger cubs make a squeaky chattering sound.

Badgers move around woods and fields quietly, but make the occasional grunt or growl.

Movement

Badgers have four limbs, each of which ends in a paw with five claws. They can walk, run, climb and even swim.

The skeleton

The badger has an internal skeleton made up of many bones. The skeleton supports and protects the body. Bones are connected to each other at joints, for example the badger's elbow and shoulder joints.

Badgers can clamber over low walls and fallen tree trunks. Young badgers can even climb low branches of trees.

Badgers don't like water, but if necessary, they can swim across ponds and rivers.

ANIMAL **FACTS**

▶ *People used to say that badgers had legs that were shorter on one side than the other. They don't! People may have believed this because they often saw badgers walking on sloping ground on the sides of hills.*

A badger's muscles

Bones cannot move on their own. They are moved by muscles, which are attached to the bones. When a muscle contracts, or gets shorter, it pulls on the bone and moves it. Badgers have strong leg muscles to help them run and dig.

Daily life

The badger is an incredibly clean animal. Each day it spends time grooming its hair and cleaning the sett.

Keeping clean

Badgers like to keep their setts free of droppings. They go to the toilet in a group of shallow pits, called a latrine, some distance from the sett. When the cubs first leave the sett they learn to follow their mother to use the latrine. A badger grooms its hair each day. It uses its teeth to remove dirt and parasites.

ANIMAL **FACTS**

▶ *A latrine consists of up to 50 pits, each 10 cm deep and covering an area of between 2 and 5 sq m.*

Grooming is very important as it keeps the hair clean.

This badger has collected fresh bedding and is pulling it backwards into the sett.

Housework

Badgers line their chambers with bedding such as moss, straw, bracken and dry leaves. They change this bedding frequently. The old bedding is pulled out of the tunnel and left close to the entrance. Clean dry bedding is important in the nursery chamber. A thick layer of bedding insulates the cubs from the cold soil underneath them and keeps out cold draughts.

animal
CLUES

Once you have found a badger sett, look for the latrine. This will be a short distance from an entrance and will look like a group of shallow pits dug in the ground.

Surviving winter

During the winter months, the weather is cold and the days are short. There is little food around, so badgers spend most of the winter sleeping in their setts.

Preparing for winter

During the autumn months, badgers eat a lot of food, especially blackberries and fallen apples. They build up the fat in their bodies and put on weight. This helps them to survive the winter. Also they collect plenty of fresh bedding for the sett.

These badgers are sniffing for food in fallen leaves. It is very important for young badgers to build up fat before their first winter. If they are not large enough they may not survive until spring.

These young badgers will spend most of the winter in their sett.

science **LINKS**

A number of British mammals, for example hedgehogs, hibernate. Find out which British mammals hibernate. Where do they hibernate and for how long?

Badgers sleep in winter

Many small mammals such as dormice and hedgehogs hibernate in winter. They go into a deep sleep for winter, not stirring from their resting place. Badgers do not hibernate but they do spend a lot of time sleeping. They eat very little and have to survive on their body fat. This means that they gradually lose weight over the winter. They emerge each night to use the latrine and find fresh bedding.

Badger stories

Keeping traditions

In old British stories, the badger is considered to be a steady, determined and home-loving animal. The badger is thought to be a 'keeper of traditions' since many generations of badgers have lived in the same sett, each badger adding to and improving the sett and passing it on to their offspring. They stick to the same paths for many years, and they continue to use them even if part of the path is blocked by a road or new house. In Scotland, the badger is admired for its courage and power. Sometimes the Scots wear sporrans (the purse worn with traditional Highland dress) made from badger hair.

'The Wind in the Willows'

The book *The Wind in the Willows* features many animals that live by the river and in the Wild Wood. One of the characters is a badger. In the story, the badger is a quiet animal who tries to maintain law and order in the wood. He is kind and generous although he can be a bit stern at times. The other animals of the wood respect him and some are even scared of him.

Badger facts

Badger relations
There are nine species or types of badger in the world, including the American badger. The badger's closest relatives are weasels, stoats, wolverines and otters.

Did you know...?
The old English word for badger is 'brocc' and this word appears in many place names, for example Brockenhurst in Hampshire and Brockhall in Northamptonshire.

MAIN FEATURES OF THE BADGER

- *The badger is a mammal.*
- *It lives in a family group called a clan.*
- *It is found mostly in woodland, on farmland and in towns and cities.*
- *Its home is called a sett.*
- *The sow gives birth to two or three cubs in spring.*
- *The badger is an omnivore.*

Badger websites
Badgers on the Web
www.badgers.org.uk
Website with good links together with useful fact pages and photos.

National Federation of Badger Groups
www.nfbg.org.uk
Website giving valuable information about how to watch badgers in the wild.

The Mammal Society
www.mammal.org.uk/badger.htm
Website providing information on the badger and all the other mammals that are found in Britain.

Note to parents and teachers
Every effort has been made by the publishers to ensure that these websites are suitable for children, that they are of the highest educational value, and that they contain no inappropriate or offensive material. However, because of the nature of the Internet, it is impossible to guarantee that the contents of these sites will not be altered. We strongly advise that Internet access is supervised by a responsible adult.

Glossary

boar a male badger

carnivore an animal that eats only meat

clan a family group of badgers, living together

cub a young badger

gland a group of cells that produce a liquid, similar to sweat glands in the skin

habitat the place where an animal lives

hibernate go into a deep sleep for the winter months

latrine a group of shallow pits close to a sett, used by the badgers as a toilet

mammal an animal that usually gives birth to live young. The female mammal produces milk for her young

mate reproduce

nocturnal animals that are nocturnal are active at night and rest during the day

omnivore an animal that eats a mixed diet of plants and meat

parasite an animal or plant that lives on another animal or plant causing harm, for example a flea or a tick

pregnancy the period of being pregnant. A female animal is pregnant when she has a baby or babies developing inside her

sett the home of a badger, with underground tunnels and chambers

sow a female badger

territory the range or area of land in which an animal lives

wolverine a short-legged carnivorous mammal, found in Alaska, Northern Canada, Scandinavia and Siberia

Index